BBC earth

DO YOU KNOW?

Level 1

ANIMAL FAMILIES

Inspired by BBC Earth TV series and developed with input from BBC Earth natural history specialists

Written by Camilla de la Bedoyere
Text adapted by Nick Coates
Series Editor: Nick Coates

LADYBIRD BOOKS

UK | USA | Canada | Ireland | Australia
India | New Zealand | South Africa

Ladybird Books is part of the Penguin Random House group of companies
whose addresses can be found at global.penguinrandomhouse.com.
www.penguin.co.uk   www.puffin.co.uk   www.ladybird.co.uk

Penguin
Random House
UK

First published 2020
001

Contents

New words

carry

grandmother

grow

hug
(noun and verb)

insect

kiss
(verb)

leaf
(leaves)

look after

look like

sleepy

What is a family?

Families can have mothers, fathers, children and babies. Mothers and fathers **look after** babies and children.

This is a big family of monkeys.

The big monkeys look after the baby monkeys.

These are animal families, too.

Watch the video (see page 32).
What is the young monkey doing?
Is the baby happy?

What are baby animals called?

All animals have babies.

A baby elephant is a calf.

A baby dolphin is a calf, too.

A baby lion is a cub.

A baby bear is a cub, too.

FIND OUT!

Use books or the internet to find out the names of these baby animals:
a) pig   b) sheep   c) cat

Do you know these babies?

A baby dog is a pup.

A baby meerkat is a pup, too.

A baby kangaroo is a joey.

A baby zebra is a foal.

A baby horse is a foal, too.

PROJECT

Work in a group.
Make a list of animals and their babies.
Talk about your favourite baby animal.

What is in an egg?

A baby bird is in an egg!

The egg opens.

There is a baby bird.
It is small.

A baby bird is a chick.

This penguin has two chicks.

▶ WATCH!

Watch the video (see page 32).
Look at the chicks. What colour are they?
What colour are the mother and father?

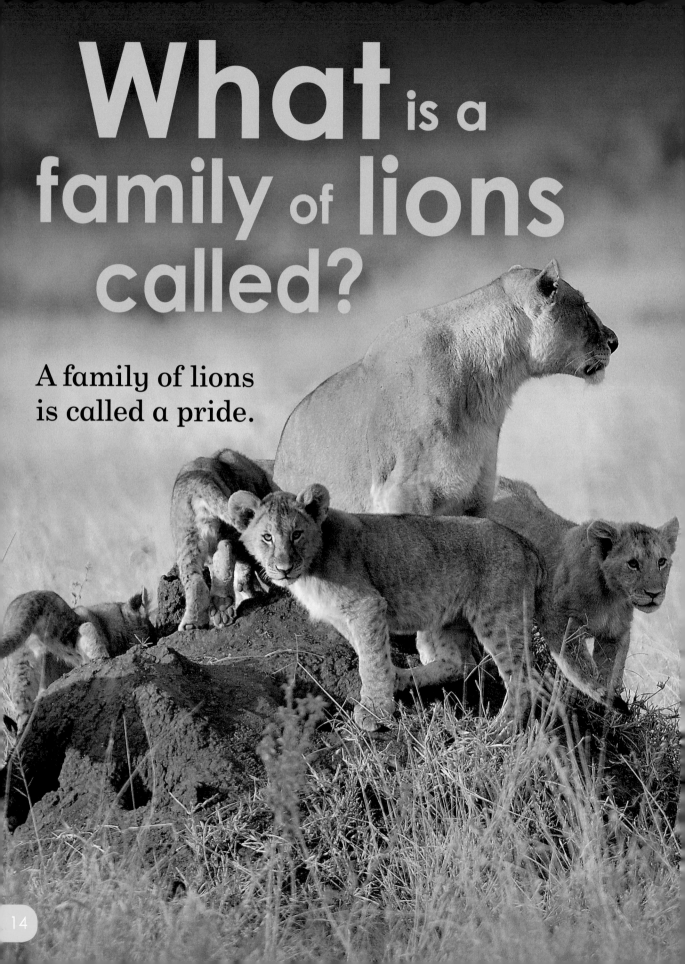

What is a family of lions called?

A family of lions is called a pride.

There is one father in a pride. He is a big lion.

mane

A mother lion is a lioness.

There can be lots of lionesses and cubs in a pride.

LOOK!

Look at the pages.
Do mother lions have manes?
What is a baby lion called?

Who looks after baby lions?

Mother lions look after the cubs.

This lioness is **carrying** her cub.

The father can look after the cubs, too.

This father is **sleepy**!

WATCH!

Watch the video (see page 32).
How many lion cubs can you see?

Do fathers look after eggs?

Some baby animals **grow** in eggs. These fathers look after the eggs.

Baby frogs are tadpoles.
They grow in eggs.

This father frog
looks after the eggs.

A seadragon is a fish.

This seadragon has red eggs.
He looks after the eggs.

eggs

FIND OUT!

Use books or the internet to find out
what a tadpole looks like when it
comes out of the egg.

Do babies look like their mothers?

Some babies **look like** their mother or their father.

Does this baby zebra look like its mother?

Some babies do not look like their mother or their father.

Does this baby bird look like its mother?

LOOK!

Look at the pages.
Can you see a mane on the zebra's neck?
How many legs does a bird have?

What do baby animals eat?

Some baby animals drink milk.

The mother makes milk for her baby.

This baby whale drinks milk.

A baby whale is a calf.

Some baby animals eat fish.

This puffin has fish for his chick.

PROJECT

Work in a group.
Find out what these baby animals eat:
a) duckling   b) caterpillar   c) joey

A baby meerkat eats **insects**. They also eat scorpions.

This mother helps her baby eat a scorpion.

scorpion

Baby meerkats and baby bonobos learn to find food.

A bonobo helps her baby find good **leaves**.

This baby bonobo eats leaves.

THINK!

What do you learn from your family?

Who has a grandmother?

Baby elephants have **grandmothers!**

The grandmother looks after the family. She is big and old.

An elephant family is a herd.

This calf is sleepy!

LOOK!

Look at the pages.
Who looks after the elephant family?

Who likes hugs?

We do, and some animals do, too!

A mother sloth **hugs** her baby.

This baby sloth looks like its mother.

Chimps like to hug.
They like to **kiss**, too!

This mother chimp kisses her baby.

PROJECT

Work in a group.
Find your favourite animal in the book.
Draw a picture of the animal.
Write its name.

Quiz

Choose the correct answers.

1 A baby bear is . . .
  a a calf.
  b a cub.

2 A joey is a baby . . .
  a kangaroo.
  b zebra.

3 A family of lions
is called . . .
a a pride.
b a lioness.

4 A puffin eats . . .
a leaves.
b fish.

5 Who looks after this
baby elephant?
a its father
b its grandmother

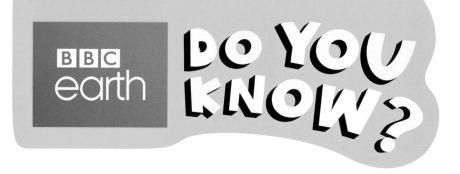

Visit www.ladybirdeducation.co.uk for
FREE **DO YOU KNOW?** teaching resources.

- video clips with simplified voiceover and subtitles
- video and comprehension activities
- class projects and lesson plans
- audio recording of every book
- digital version of every book
- full answer keys

To access video clips, audio tracks and digital books:

1 Go to **www.ladybirdeducation.co.uk**
2 Click "Unlock book"
3 Enter the code below

arm07VWtat

Stay safe online! Some of the DO YOU KNOW? activities ask children to do extra research online. Remember:

- ensure an adult is supervising;
- use established search engines such as Google or Kiddle;
- children should never share personal details, such as name, home or school address, telephone number or photos.